Original title:

Winter's Whispering Winds

Author: Thor Castlebury

ISBN HARDBACK: 978-9916-85-788-5

ISBN PAPERBACK: 978-9916-85-789-2

Snowflakes Dancing in the Gale

Whispers of winter weave through the air,
Snowflakes twirl, like dreams beyond compare.
In swirling patterns, they chase and they play,
A symphony of silence in the heart of the day.

Each flake a wonder, a moment set free,
They pirouette softly on the breath of the tree.
The world is transformed in this icy ballet,
As twilight beckons, bidding night to array.

Shadows of the Silent Frost

In the hush of the night, where shadows reside,
The frost paints the earth, like a moonlit guide.
Traces of silver, each blade wrapped in light,
A canvas of stillness, where dreams meet the
night.

Beneath the pale glow of a starlit embrace,
The whispers of winter declare their soft grace.
Silent and gentle, the world seems to freeze,
Where echoes of warmth blend with the chill of
the breeze.

Breath of Icy Dreams

A breath of the night holds the chill of our sighs,
Each moment suspended beneath velvet skies.
The air is adorned with the shimmer of stars,
In this frozen realm, we forget all our scars.

Close your eyes gently, let the stillness surround,
Embrace the soft whispers where magic is found.

In the heart of the frost lies a dreamer's retreat,
Where icy reflections and warm memories meet.

The Lullaby of Frosted Pines

Under the boughs where the soft snow lays,
The pines hum a lullaby, in quiet displays.
Resonant whispers through the frosted tips,
Each note a reminder of nature's sweet grips.

As twilight descends, their silhouettes sway,
Murmuring secrets of the close of the day.
Wrapped in a shroud of this silvery sheen,
The world finds its rest in the calm and serene.

Soft Airs Wrapped in Snow

Soft airs whisper through the trees,
Carrying secrets of winter's freeze.
Beneath the blanket, silence hums,
As gentle flurries dance and come.

Each flake a memory softly spun,
In the quiet embrace of the setting sun.
A world transformed, pristine and bright,
As shadows mingle with soft white light.

Drifted Dreams of the Cold

In dreams that drift like snowflakes fly,
We wander through the frosty sky.
Wrapped in a cloak of shimmering light,
We chase the stars in the dark of night.

Each breath a mist, each moment slow,
Painting our hopes on a canvas of snow.
As time stands still in the chill of the air,
We find our hearts within moments rare.

Gales Carrying Faint Reminders

Gales carry whispers from days gone by,
Echoing laughter, a low, soft sigh.
Through winter's breath, the past draws near,
In the rustling leaves, we glimpse the year.

Faint reminders flutter like pages of time,
Tales in the wind, a forgotten rhyme.
With every gust, stories unfold,
Of cherished moments, and dreams retold.

Murmuring Magic in the Frozen Air

Amidst the stillness, magic unfolds,
In whispered secrets that winter holds.
The breath of nature, a gentle sigh,
As snowflakes dance in a frozen sky.

Murmuring tales of an unseen grace,
Each frozen moment, a soft embrace.
In the air, a symphony sweetly plays,
Binding our hearts in winter's gaze.

Shadows of Silent Discovery

In twilight's hush, where whispers dwell,
Shadows dance like stories to tell.
With every step on the emerald moss,
Secrets unfold, no matter the cost.

Beneath the veil of the ancient trees,
Nature breathes with a gentle tease.
Each rustling leaf, a guiding hand,
Leading souls to forgotten lands.

Murmurs of the Cold Moonlight

The moon hangs low, a silver spray,
Murmurs echo where shadows play.
In the stillness, dreams take flight,
Kisses of night beneath cold light.

Whispers of stars, secrets untold,
A tapestry woven from stories old.
In the pale glow, hearts intertwine,
Journeying through the divine design.

Sip of Frosty Memories

In a cup of warmth, the frost does gleam,
Each sip a portal to a distant dream.
Memories linger in the winter air,
Chasing echoes, a tender affair.

Snowflakes drift like thoughts unspoken,
In the chill, soft moments broken.
The taste of nostalgia, rich and bold,
Whispers of stories waiting to be told.

The Stillness of Flurries

In the quiet realm where the flurries fall,
The world is hushed, wrapped in a shawl.
Each flake a whisper, soft and clear,
Filling the heart with calmness near.

Stillness cradles the night so deep,
As nature sighs and the earth does sleep.
Moments freeze in a crystal embrace,
Time stands still in this sacred space.

Hints of Chill Beneath the Stars

In the night where whispers roam,
Chilled breezes weave like threads of foam,
Underneath the astral glow,
Secrets of the winter sow.

Frosty sighs slip through the pines,
Tracing patterns in the lines,
Of shimmering light that glistens near,
Hints of chill, a guide so clear.

Each step crunches on the ground,
As starlit silence wraps around,
Nature slumbers, soft and deep,
In dreams where winter shadows creep.

The cosmos winks in frosty hues,
A soft reminder in the blues,
Hints of chill beneath the skies,
In winter's grasp, the heart complies.

Echoing Breath of the Cold

In the twilight, comes the sigh,
Of winter's breath that flits and flies,
Over hills where silence falls,
Echoing through nature's walls.

Puffing clouds of frosty air,
Trace the dusk with tender care,
Crickets hush, their song now ceased,
In the cradle of the beast.

Every flake a whispered thought,
In the web of time, it's caught,
Echoing what the heart believes,
In the dance of frosted leaves.

From the mountains to the vale,
Stories of the cold regale,
The echoing breath sings nearby,
A lullaby beneath the sky.

A Symphony of Frozen Whispers

In the stillness, notes take flight,
A symphony in crisp twilight,
Whispers tangled in the trees,
Melodies entwined with the breeze.

Each flake a silent lullaby,
As they glide and gently sigh,
Frosted vocals fill the air,
Nature plays her tune with care.

The night unfolds its icy sheet,
With every sound, a pulse, a beat,
As echoes swirl in rhythmic grace,
A frozen song in winter's embrace.

Listen close, let silence reign,
In this haven, joy and pain,
A symphony 'neath the pale glow,
Of winter's heart, a tranquil show.

Soft Crystals in the Air

Dancing lightly, crystals fall,
Adorning trees, as night does call,
Whispers caught in icy lace,
Softly draping nature's face.

Glistening jewels on branches freeze,
Breath of winter in the breeze,
A tapestry of sparkling light,
Transforming shadows into bright.

With every gust, they swirl and twirl,
Creating magic, an icy whirl,
Soft crystals linger, twinkling fair,
An ephemeral touch in the air.

As dawn approaches, glimmers fade,
Yet in each heart, the wonders laid,
Soft crystals in the world bestow,
A fleeting glimpse of winter's glow.

Glistening Whispers of the North

In the twilight glow where the fir trees lean,
Glistening whispers weave tales unseen.
Snowflakes flutter like dreams in the air,
Crystals of silence, a beauty so rare.

Underneath blankets of pure, shimmering white,
The heartbeats of winter echo softly at night.
Frost-kissed winds carry secrets untold,
Stories of warmth in the chill, brave and bold.

A chorus of stars twinkles overhead,
Each one a wonder, a wish left unsaid.
Nature's embrace wraps the world with a sigh,
In the glisten of snow, where the moments drift
by.

Secrets From the Icy Realms

Deep within glaciers, where shadows play,
Secrets awaken in the light of the day.
Frozen whispers glide over rocks and streams,
Guardians of time, cradling ancient dreams.

Each crack of the ice tells a story profound,
Echoes of epochs, where silence is found.
What once was a river now sighs in retreat,
Woven in stillness, a tale bittersweet.

Softly, the winter unveils its disguise,
A dance of pure silence beneath cloudy skies.
Nature's own secret, in sparkles and beams,
Lies hidden in shadows, alive with our dreams.

Ethereal Voices in the Snow

Through fields of white, where the wild winds
race,
Ethereal voices whisper with grace.
Hushed are the echoes of days long ago,
In the depths of the winter, the stories still flow.

Footprints etched softly on pure frosted ground,
Carried on breezes, a melodic sound.
Each flake a messenger sent from above,
Filling the silence with warmth and with love.

The moon casts a glow on this tranquil expanse,
As the clouds swirl and sway in a ghostly dance.
Nature cradles the night with a blanket of dreams,

In the whispers of snow, it endlessly seems.

Shadows of Shivering Nonsense

In the shadowy corners where the cold winds
moan,
Lies a tale of nonsense, in whispers alone.
Icicles dangle like guardians of lore,
While the frost turns the world into something
much more.

Laughter erupts from a snowman's bright hat,
As the snowflakes conspire in playful combat.
The trees chuckle low, their branches entwined,
In the symphony of winter, joyfully unconfined.

Shivering nonsense skips through the air,
With a wink and a twist, its magic laid bare.
In the depths of the night, where shadows take
flight,
Winter weaves laughter through the blanket of
white.

The Serenity of Cold Nights

In the stillness of the moonlit night,
Stars shimmer softly, a celestial sight,
Blankets of silence drape the earth,
Whispers of peace, a gentle rebirth.

Frosty air wraps the world in white,
Each breath a cloud in the tranquil night,
Time slows down in the winter's embrace,
Nature holds secrets in a shimmering space.

Frost's Breath on the Wind

Winter whispers through branches bare,
Frost's breath dances in the crisp night air,
Each flake, a jewel that sparkles and spins,
Painting the landscape where quiet begins.

The trees stand tall, dressed in icy gown,
Guardians of peace in a snow-laden town,
A lullaby murmurs, the wind softly sighs,
As the world settles under starlit skies.

Hushed Moments in the Frozen Glade

In the heart of the glade where the shadows play,
Winter's breath hushes the world for the day,
Each flurry a dream that settles with care,
Crystals of time hang lightly in the air.

The soft crunch of snow beneath quiet feet,
Nature holds still, where the earth and sky meet,
A soft glow emerges, as twilight descends,
In hushed moments of magic, the evening mends.

Lullabies of the Silent Breeze

Among the pines, the air sings low,
Lullabies of winter in whispers flow,
A melody carried on the evening chill,
Caressing the senses, a magic to fill.

Each branch adorned with crystalline grace,
Creates a symphony in nature's embrace,
The silent breeze, a tender refrain,
In the stillness of night, peace shall remain.

Shadows Weaving Through Snowy Pines

Beneath the boughs where silence sings,
Shadows dance with whispered wings.
A tapestry of night unfolds,
As secrets of the forest hold.

Moonlight drapes in silver threads,
Over dreams where stillness treads.
Pines stand tall in frosty grace,
Guardians of this tranquil place.

Driftwood Dreams Beneath the Pale Moon.

On shores where time and tide align,
Driftwood stories twist and twine.
The moon hangs low, a watchful eye,
As dreams are cast upon the sky.

Waves whisper secrets to the sand,
Carving tales from a gentle hand.
In the soft glow of night's embrace,
Driftwood dreams find their perfect space.

Frosted Echoes of Silence

In the stillness, frost takes flight,
Painting whispers on the night.
Echoes linger, soft and sweet,
Nature's breath in soft retreat.

Each flake a note, pure and bright,
Melodies born from winter's light.
In this hush where moments freeze,
Silence sings upon the breeze.

Veil of Crystal Breezes

A veil of crystals drapes the land,
Glistening gems in winter's hand.
Breezes carry a tender chill,
Whispers of dreams that time will fulfill.

Through frosted branches, laughter flows,
As nature wraps in soft repose.
Each breath of wind, a gentle sigh,
Weaving magic in the sky.

Serene Chill of the Twilight Air

In the quiet dusk, where shadows play,
The twilight air whispers secrets of the day.
Stars emerge in the velvet sky,
Breathing life into dreams that high abide.

Coolness wraps the earth in a gentle embrace,
As moonlight dances with elegant grace.
Nature holds its breath, a moment so rare,
In the serene chill of the twilight air.

Frosted Petals on the Wind

Delicate blooms clad in crystalline white,
Drifting softly like whispers in the night.
The chill of winter cradles their essence,
As frost-kissed petals tell tales of persistence.

With each gentle gust, they twirl and they sway,
A ballet of beauty, a fleeting display.
Nature's brush paints with silver and blue,
Frosted petals on the wind, a dream come true.

Ethereal Hush of the Long Night

Wrapped in silence, the world holds its breath,
An ethereal hush, where time dances with death.
The stars are confessions of secrets untold,
Illuminating the stillness, so calm and so bold.

Moonbeams weave stories through shadows so
deep,
In the long night's embrace, the mysteries sleep.
Nature unveils its timeless delight,
In the ethereal hush of the long night.

The Symphony of Shimmering Frost

In the still of the morn, where the world glistens
bright,
The shimmering frost wraps the earth in pure
light.
A symphony whispers, each note soft and clear,
Nature's magic resounding, a sound to revere.

Crystals awaken at dawn's gentle call,
Every blade, every branch, a masterpiece tall.
The cold air vibrates with harmonies grand,
In the symphony of shimmering frost, we stand.

Hushed Conversations in the Cold

In the stillness of the midnight hour,
Echoes linger, softly weave,
Chilled breath dances, a fleeting flower,
Silent secrets we both believe.

Snowflakes whisper with every fall,
Muffled words wrapped in white,
The trees stand guard, timeless and tall,
Holding our stories, hidden from light.

Voices carried on the frosty air,
Melodies blend with the winter's sigh,
A tapestry woven in moments rare,
As night deepens, our hopes take flight.

In this sanctuary, hearts lay bare,
Frozen echoes twine in the cold,
Lost in the magic of deep, still air,
Our whispered dreams softly unfold.

Whispered Dreams Beneath Frosted Stars

Underneath a blanket of frosted skies,
Where the stars twinkle like scattered pearls,
Whispers of dreams take ancient guise,
In the hush of night, our spirit unfurls.

The moon, a guardian, shines with grace,
Guiding our thoughts through the powdery night,

With every secret, we carve a space,
Where wishes ignite in twinkling light.

Frost-kissed dreams weave like a trance,
Every sigh shared, a tale to impart,
In the quiet, we find our dance,
Our hopes trace the heavens, mapping the heart.

So let the cool air cradle our fears,
As frost transforms shadows to golden gleam,
Each whispered thought, a treasure appears,
Crafting our futures with delicate dream.

Serenade of the Northern Breeze

In the north, where the chilly winds sing,
Nature's voice shimmers with a light hush,
Branches sway, and the night takes wing,
As the world slumbers in a silvered rush.

The breeze carries tales from distant lands,
Rustling through pines, it weaves its tune,
With every gentlest touch, it understands,
A secret symphony, under the moon.

In each cool sigh, memories float free,
Harmonies dance with the silent snow,
Together we dream, just you and me,
As the northern breeze whispers low.

Stars blink in sync with the night's ballet,
Drawing us close in this cocoon divine,
With every breeze, our worries decay,
In the serenade where your heart meets mine.

Quiet Reflections in the Frost

In the morning light, the frost glistens bright,
Mirroring truths in a crystalline gaze,
Every breath inhaled, a moment of flight,
Reflecting the dreams of our yesterdays.

Stillness blankets the world in repose,
Nature's canvas, a delicate art,
In each frozen shard, a story grows,
As quiet reflections whisper the heart.

Time pauses, lost in this gentle space,
Where the chill hugs close, yet warms the soul,
Searching for solace in nature's embrace,
Finding our place in the universe whole.

So let us linger in this frosty dawn,
Where silence holds the pulse of our fate,
In quiet reflections, we're never truly gone,
Each moment cherished, serene and ornate.

Breezes Carried by Ice

In a realm where silence reigns,
Breezes whisper 'neath the chill,
Carried forth on icy chains,
Nature's breath, an artful thrill.

Trees adorned with crystal lace,
Glistening under winter's song,
Each gust, a fleeting embrace,
In frozen stillness, we belong.

The rivers stretch in silver dreams,
Reflecting moonlight's tender gaze,
In this stillness, time redeems,
A dance of frost, where spirits blaze.

Echoes of a season passed,
Whirling leaves in a gentle flight,
Leaving memories amassed,
In breezes carried by the night.

Soft Shivers in the Night

Under a blanket of starlit skies,
Soft shivers flutter, timid and bright,
Whispers of shadows, where mystery lies,
In the still of the deep, quiet night.

The moon hangs low, a watchful eye,
Casting its glow on secrets untold,
Where dreams take flight, and spirits sigh,
Embracing the world in a cloak of cold.

Every breath a chilling caress,
As thoughts dance lightly in twilight's thrill,
In the heart of silence, we find our rest,
Soft shivers awaken the night's gentle chill.

Wrapped in the hush of a velvet theme,
We wade through echoes of thought and lore,
Each moment alive, like a fleeting dream,
Soft shivers linger, forevermore.

Frost's Delicate Embrace

With dawn's arrival, a canvas anew,
Frost paints the world in shimmering white,
A delicate embrace, tender and true,
Where beauty is born from the heart of night.

Each blade of grass, a jewel in disguise,
Captured light as if a fleeting glance,
Nature smiles with crystalline eyes,
Inviting the morn to join in the dance.

Branches bow under the weight of dreams,
Wrapped in gossamer threads that gleam,
Frost's gentle hand, a whisper that seems,
To echo the pulse of life's quiet stream.

In every corner, a story unfolds,
Of warmth found in winter's tender grace,
As the sun ascends, and the chill it holds,
Melds into the promise of a warm embrace.

Ghostly Murmurs in the Dark

In the stillness, a silence profound,
Ghostly murmurs weave through the trees,
Carried softly, without a sound,
Like secrets carried on the evening breeze.

Echoes of laughter from days gone by,
Dance in shadows, elusive and bright,
As the night sky unfurls, an endless sigh,
Where echoes of dreams take flight.

Each whisper a story, a fleeting trace,
Of lives once lived, now shadows dim,
Their spirits linger, a warm embrace,
Filling the darkness where memories swim.

Through the veil of night, we beckon and seek,
Those ghostly murmurs that never depart,
In the hush of the dark, the lost souls speak,
Unraveling threads deep within the heart.

Celestial Serenade of the Frost

Underneath the starlit dome so bright,
Frost weaves its silver threads of light,
Whispers of winter dance in the air,
As celestial notes fall soft, laid bare.

The moon ignites the craters below,
A serenade of silence, soft and slow,
Each flake a song, a story untold,
In a tapestry woven of shimmering gold.

The Alchemy of Ice and Wind

Where breath of winter kisses the ground,
The alchemy of ice in whispers profound,
Frozen cauldrons brew tempestuous dreams,
As the world shimmers in crystalline beams.

Winds weave through branches with a playful
grace,
Transforming the landscape, a magical space,
In the crucible of cold, wonders unfold,
Creating an art that is precious and bold.

Enigmatic Shivers of the Evening

When twilight hushes the vibrant day,
Enigmatic shivers begin to sway,
Mysteries cloaked in shadows so deep,
Nature's secrets awaken from sleep.

The chill of night wraps around the trees,
Each breath of air sings soft melodies,
Echoes of whispers from ages gone by,
Under the veil of a darkened sky.

Whispering Shadows of the Poles

In the land where silence paints the scene,
Whispering shadows dance like spirits unseen,
Soft echoes of ancient glaciers stand tall,
As the icy expanse greets the night's call.

Beneath the auroras that shimmer and sway,
Time folds in layers where memories lay,
Polar secrets bated, breathed in the frost,
In the realm where light and shadow are tossed.

Echoes of the Chill

In the quiet nooks where shadows dwell,
Frosted breath weaves a curious spell,
Night blankets whispers, cold and profound,
Echoes of chill in the stillness abound.

Moonlight glimmers on the frozen lake,
Each ripple a secret that the night does make,
Voices entwined in the whispering breeze,
Carried on pathways through stark winter trees.

Crystal Whispers Beneath the Sky

Beneath the vast dome where the stars softly play,

Crystal whispers dance in the silver ray,
Nature's soft laughter, a tender embrace,
Glistening dreams in the moon's tender grace.

Each droplet of dew holds a tale to be spun,
A soft serenade as the day is undone,
Shimmering secrets weave through the night,
In the heart of the stillness, hearts take flight.

Winds Sighing Frosty Tales

Winds sigh softly with frigid delight,
Carrying stories from the depths of the night,
Breezes that whisper of seasons long past,
Fragments of moments forever amassed.

Branches sway gently in a soft, icy waltz,
Echoing tales of nature's faults,
With each gust, the world takes a breath,
In the chill of the night, we find life and death.

The Algorithm of Icewhisper

In the labyrinth of frost where silence grows deep,

Lies an algorithm of secrets we keep,
Each crystalline flake a code yet untold,
Whispers of winter in patterns unfold.

Mathematics of nature in coldness aligned,
An elegant rhythm, so perfectly timed,
Notes of the frost dance in numeric refrain,
The language of ice in a world so arcane.

Frosty Embrace of the Night

In the stillness, shadows play,
Where whispers of the moonlight sway,
A blanket wrapped in silver hue,
The world, a canvas cold and new.

Stars blink down with frosted gaze,
Guide the wanderers through the haze,
Each breath a cloud, ephemeral light,
Caught in the frosty embrace of night.

The silent trees in shivers stand,
Graffiti etched by nature's hand,
A symphony of quiet grace,
In winter's arms, we find our place.

With hearts aglow in chilly cheer,
We dance with dreams, we shed our fear,
For in the dark, a spark ignites,
Enveloped in the frosty nights.

Chilling Echoes in the Silence

In the depth of winter's pause,
The world awaits, caught in a cause,
Chilling echoes resonate and swell,
A frosty chant, a whispered spell.

Through barren branches, secrets weave,
Tales of frost that humbly grieve,
Yet in their sorrow, there's a song,
A melody that feels so strong.

With each exhale, the echoes play,
In bitter winds that twist and sway,
An urging calm that chills the bone,
Where silence sings, we're never alone.

Each lingering breath rides the breeze,
Chilling echoes that bring us peace,
Within the void, a gentle call,
In the silent night, we hear it all.

Breath of the Icy Gale

Whispers ride on the breath of gales,
Carrying stories where silence prevails,
In every gust, a thousand tales,
Of rivers frozen and winter's trails.

Frosty fingers, they caress the land,
Painting landscapes, both stern and grand,
An artist clad in icy attire,
Stirring the heart with winter's fire.

The howl of the wind, a mournful song,
Echoes of nature, where we belong,
We find our courage in the chill,
As every breath is a test of will.

Through nighttime's cloak, the gales will play,
Guiding our footsteps along the way,
With each icy caress, we unveil,
The beauty found in the breath of the gale.

Secrets of the Snow-Kissed Air

Whispers linger in the snow-kissed air,
Secrets hidden, a world laid bare,
Each flake a story, a time held tight,
In winter's grasp, cloaked in pure white.

Frozen whispers cradle the earth,
Glimmers of wonder, of ancient birth,
A tapestry woven with threads of chill,
In every sigh, the quiet thrills.

In twilight's glow, the landscape gleams,
Reflecting softly our chilled dreams,
Each heartbeat echoes the silent lore,
Of nature's breath, we yearn for more.

As shadows stretch and silence mutes,
We lean into the warmth of subtle roots,
For in the cold, we find it clear,
The secrets whispered, we hold near.

The Calm of Snowy Emptiness

In silver blankets, silence drapes,
Fluttering softly, the world escapes,
Each flake a hush, a drifting sigh,
Where time stands still, and dreams can fly.

The trees wear coats of glistening white,
Beneath their branches, shadows slight,
Footprints fade, like whispers of night,
In the calm of snowy, serene delight.

Distant mountains wrapped in repose,
In nature's stillness, our heartbeats close,
With every breath, the cold air ignites,
A tranquil canvas, a dance of lights.

So let us wander through this frozen land,
Hand in hand, with warmth so grand,
In the calm of snowy, sacred stillness,
We find the beauty of tranquil fullness.

Secrets of the Frostbound Spirits

In the mist where shadows play,
Ancient secrets drift and sway,
Frostbound spirits, silent in their grace,
Guarding whispers in nature's embrace.

Icicles hang like frozen dreams,
Glittering softly in moonlit beams,
Each sparkle tells a tale untold,
Of winter's magic, a legend old.

A shiver runs through trees so high,
As spirits waltz, with stars they fly,
In the chill of night, they weave and spin,
A tapestry of frost, where stories begin.

Listen closely to the wind's refrain,
It carries secrets wrapped in the pain,
Of seasons past, where echoes dwell,
In the frostbound spirits, their stories swell.

Celestial Whispers in the Chill

Underneath the velvet sky,
Stars come forth, like dreams that fly,
Their whispers dance through the icy night,
Celestial secrets, pure and bright.

The moon glows softly, a silver guide,
In the quietude, where mysteries hide,
Each twinkling glint a gentle call,
To hearts that wander, to souls that fall.

A hush envelops the earthly realm,
While cosmic forces take the helm,
In every breath, a starlit thrill,
Celestial whispers in the chill.

As frost weaves lace on branches bare,
Nature invokes a silent prayer,
For in this moment, we are one,
With the cosmos vast, and the winter sun.

Frosted Heartbeats in the Night

Thumping slowly, the world's heartbeat,
Wrapped in frost, where dreamers meet,
Each chill a pulse, a tender sound,
In snowy blankets, our hopes abound.

The night air crackles with sparkling peace,
As time stands still, and worries cease,
Frosted memories dance like fire,
Kindled warmth in our hearts' desire.

With each step, the snowflakes sigh,
Cradling whispers of love nearby,
In the night, where shadows play,
Frosted heartbeats guide the way.

Embraced by winter's soft caress,
We find our solace, our happiness,
In frozen moments, forever tight,
Connected deeply, in the night.

Frostbitten Secrets of the Hearth

In the glow of embers, whispers dwell,
Frostbitten secrets that the shadows tell.
Crackling warmth wraps the night's bitter chill,
Echoes of laughter weave time, stand still.

Through windowpanes frosted, dreams softly
creep,
Memories knitted, promises we keep.
The heart of the hearth, where stories ignite,
In warmth's gentle cradle, love conquers the
night.

The Calm Before the Snowfall

A hush falls gently on the sleeping glade,
Breath of winter whispers, a tranquil cascade.
Boughs thick with promise bow low with grace,
Anticipation dances, time holds its pace.

Silhouettes linger in the softening light,
Nature's deep slumber prepares for the white.
Each moment suspended, a world waits in peace,
For nature's white blanket, a sweet, soft release.

Voices of the Frostbitten Night

Under the vastness of a star-speckled dome,
Frostbitten whispers echo, instinctively roam.
The moonlight glimmers on the crisp, frozen air,
A chorus of silence, the night laid bare.

Each rustle of branches, a tale yet untold,
The language of winter, both tender and bold.
Shivers of secrets dance in frozen streams,
In the depths of the night, we awaken our dreams.

Charmed Silence of the Darkened Wood

Amidst the tall pines in the shadows' embrace,
A charmed silence lingers, a magical space.
Whispers of starlight, the night softly calls,
In the heart of the woods, where serenity falls.

Muffled by snowdrifts, time starts to stretch,
Branches adorned with frost, nature's sketch.
Footprints in starlight trace stories anew,
In the darkened wood where the dreams come
true.

The Secrets of Glistening Air

In the stillness where the soft winds sigh,
Glimmers dance in the twilight sky,
Whispers of dreams in a silken embrace,
Unraveling mysteries of time and space.

Beneath the stars, where shadows converge,
Glistening secrets begin to emerge,
Each breath a melody, pure and rare,
We lose ourselves in the secrets of air.

Whispers Beneath the Snow

Silent blankets cover the earth so white,
While dreams awaken in the softest night,
Beneath the snow, the world holds its breath,
Life hidden deeply, a promise of depth.

Each flake a story, each drift a sigh,
Whispers of seasons that flutter and fly,
In chilled embrace, the past does not fade,
For life is a cycle, an undying parade.

The Quietude of Icebound Nights

Moonlight glistens on the frozen shore,
A canvas of silence, forevermore,
Stars like diamonds, scattered afar,
Each moment frozen, a shimmering scar.

Whispers of winter weave through the trees,
Tales of the ancient carried by the breeze,
In the quietude, our hearts find peace,
As time stands still, and worries cease.

Frosted Twilight's Song

When twilight drapes in its frosted veil,
Colors blend where the night prevails,
A symphony hums through the chilly air,
Each note a promise, each chord a prayer.

In the stillness where the shadows reside,
The world holds secrets, no place to hide,
Frosted twilight wraps all in its throng,
As echoes of silence sing winter's song.

Frosted Lullabies of Solitude

In winter's grasp the silence grows,
A blanket soft in crystal flows,
Where whispers drift like feathered sighs,
And time slows down beneath the skies.

Each flake that falls, a tale untold,
Of dreams encased, of hearts consoled,
A world transformed in shades of white,
In frosted lullabies of night.

The moon above, a timid light,
Illuminates the tranquil sight,
While shadows dance on fields of snow,
In solitude, the heart can glow.

So close your eyes and breathe it in,
The peace that dwells where all begins,
In stillness found, let worries cease,
Embrace the frost, and find your peace.

The Unseen Dance of Frozen Air

In the hush of frosty twilight's breath,
The air weaves tales of life and death,
A ballet spun with unseen grace,
In every corner, a quiet embrace.

The trees stand tall, their branches bare,
As if to join the subtle air,
A rhythmic sway, though no one sees,
The dance performed by frozen trees.

Each shimmer caught in moonlight's kiss,
A fleeting moment, eternal bliss,
The stars glance down with tranquil care,
Observing closely the frozen air.

And in this space, where dreams may flow,
The unseen dance begins to grow,
In every shiver, a pulse so dear,
Whispers of life in the chill we hear.

Murmurs Beneath the Icy Canopy

Beneath the frost, in silence kept,
The murmurs of the earth are swept,
Through layers thick of icy grace,
Lie stories lost in winter's embrace.

The roots entwined in frozen dark,
Whisper secrets, each hidden spark,
They listen close to the cold wind's song,
In this hushed realm, where dreams belong.

A tapestry of silence spun,
Where time stands still, yet beckons fun,
Each rustle in the drifts of snow,
Murmurs of life, forever flow.

So pause awhile and lend an ear,
The whispers draw you ever near,
For in the depths, where shadows roam,
The icy canopy still calls you home.

Soft Caresses of the Frozen Dawn

As dawn awakens in shades of blue,
Soft caresses kiss the world anew,
With every ray, the frost dissolves,
And tender light around us evolves.

The sky adorned with a pastel hue,
Whispers secrets that morning drew,
New memories laced in the cool breeze,
In gentle touches, the heart finds ease.

Each blade of grass, a diamond's glow,
A canvas bright with winter's show,
As nature stirs from its silken sleep,
The frozen dawn begins to weep.

So cherish this moment, hold it tight,
For soft caresses in morning light,
Remind us all of beauty's call,
As winter wakes, we rise with the thrall.

Chilling Dreams of Frosted Light

In the hush of winter's embrace,
Dreams unfurl like gossamer lace,
Frosted visions dance through the night,
Wrapped in the glow of soft, pale light.

Starlit whispers ride on the breeze,
Carving secrets among the trees,
Echoes of laughter, forgotten and lost,
In the chilling embrace of morning's frost.

The world sleeps beneath a crystal shroud,
Soft as the snow, though the night is loud,
Flickers of warmth in the quiet remain,
In chilling dreams, we embrace the mundane.

Hearts flicker bright as stars in the dome,
With frosted whispers, we find our home,
In the stillness where wishes take flight,
Chilling dreams glow in the frosted light.

The Legend of Silent Winds

In valleys deep where shadows play,
The silent winds weave tales of gray,
Olden whispers, the spirits confide,
In rustling leaves where memories bide.

Once a time in a realm unknown,
The winds carried tales of love overthrown,
Of lovers lost in an icy embrace,
Seeking solace in this timeless place.

With each sigh that soft winds release,
Legends awaken, and hearts find peace,
Through valleys where the cold mist weaves,
The echo of love within the leaves.

Silent winds remember the songs of the past,
As the chill of the night holds dreams steadfast,
In every gust, a story unfurls,
The legend lingers in a world of pearls.

Whispers in the Frozen Twilight

As twilight whispers in colors so cold,
A tapestry glimmers of silver and gold,
Frozen echoes carry tales from above,
In the lingering twilight, we find tender love.

The stars peek through, with shimmers so bright,
Footprints of dreams in the softening night,
Whispers of warmth in a world made of ice,
Where moments of magic invite us to rise.

The sky bends low with a silken embrace,
Breath of the winter, gentle and chaste,
In frost-laden stillness, we gather our thoughts,
In whispers that linger, our hearts stay caught.

Echoing softly through this delicate scene,
Frozen twilight paints all we have seen,
With each whispered promise of warmth and
delight,
The world holds its breath in this shimmering
night.

Soft Echoes of the Icy World

In an icy realm where shadows reside,
Soft echoes linger, secrets they hide,
With every step upon frozen ground,
A symphony plays, a haunting sound.

Glistening crystals dance on the breeze,
Whispers of winter, tender and frail,
Each note a memory, each sound a tale,
In the icy world, where silence agrees.

The mountains stand guard, stoic and bold,
With glimmers of hope in their hearts made of
gold,
As the world swathes itself in snowy white,
Soft echoes linger into the night.

And in the stillness, we find our way,
Through echoes of dreams that refuse to sway,
In the arms of the cold, we softly unfurl,
And dance through the silence of the icy world.

A Symphony of Snowflakes and Shadows

In silence, whispers drift from skies,
A dance of flakes, where softness lies.
Each twist and turn, a fleeting flight,
They weave through shadows, painting the night.

Beneath the moon's pale, silver glow,
The world cloaked in dreams begins to slow.
In crystalline cascades, peace descends,
A symphony born where winter bends.

Each flake a note in nature's song,
Together they swirl, where hearts belong.
Through frozen branches, their laughter glides,
In this quiet ballet, serenity hides.

So let us wander, hand in hand,
Through this enchanted, white-cloaked land.
With every step, let wonders unfold,
In a symphony whispered, forever told.

Shadows in the Crystal Light

When dawn unfolds its crystal art,
Shadows stretch, then pull apart.
They dance in light, a fleeting race,
A gentle echo in this sacred space.

The world awakens, draped in calm,
With every ray, a healing balm.
Amidst the glow, lost dreams ignite,
Where shadows linger in tender light.

Each secret tucked in twilight's grasp,
Whispers of joy in nature's clasp.
The sun ascends, and shadows yield,
To the beauty of a vibrant field.

Let us wander where soft beams play,
In the realm of shadows, we find our way.
With every flicker, our souls entwine,
Illuminated hearts, forever shine.

Echoes of Solstice Stillness

In the hush of the solstice night,
The world rests, wrapped in soft twilight.
Stars glimmer like secrets, bold yet shy,
As moonbeams weave through the darkened sky.

Here lies the stillness, deep and true,
An echo of dreams that once flew.
With every breath, time gently bends,
In this sacred pause, where all transcends.

The chill of winter dances near,
Whispers of warmth, the heart holds dear.
Frozen branches, a tapestry twirls,
Nature's lullaby as night unfurls.

Together we'll weave these moments rare,
In the echo of stillness, love is bare.
With every heartbeat, the world we embrace,
In the quiet of solstice, we find our place.

Gentle Tingles of the Chilled Air

With every breath, the chill takes flight,
A gentle tingle, crisp and bright.
Winter's caress on cheeks aglow,
A whispered touch from the falling snow.

The air is filled with stories untold,
Of nights by fires, of dreams bold.
Every breezy kiss, a soft refrain,
In the dance of frost, there's no pain.

The world transformed beneath the gray,
In this serenity, we find our way.
Through whispered winds and quiet sighs,
Life slows down where the stillness lies.

So let us cherish this tranquil chill,
A gentle reminder, a heart to fill.
With every breath, in this wintry flare,
We find the magic in the chilled air.

Hushed Songs of the Frost

Beneath the silver veil of night,
The world holds its breath in tranquil light.
Each flake a note in nature's tune,
As winter's choir sings to the moon.

Silence drapes the trees so bare,
In this calm symphony, stillness rare.
Echoes dance on icy breath,
A lullaby woven through the threads of death.

Footsteps soft on glimmered ground,
In frozen dreams, where peace is found.
A melody of whispers, pure and bright,
Hushed songs echo in the frost-kissed night.

Nature's heart beats slow but strong,
In every twirl of snow, a song.
While time stands still, we softly pause,
To cherish winter's gentle cause.

Chill's Gentle Serenade

A chill descends as dusk unfolds,
Bathed in shades of lavender and gold.
The breeze, a whisper through the trees,
Sings of winter's gentle ease.

Footprints trace a silent dance,
In the crisp air, dreams dare to glance.
Every breath a cloud, soft and white,
Carried away into the night.

Stars awaken, twinkling bright,
Guiding wanderers through the night.
Their light, a balm for weary souls,
In the embrace of winter's shoals.

Each moment a treasure, fleeting fast,
Wrapped in the serenade's gentle cast.
We find our solace, hearts embrace,
In the chill's soft touch, a warm grace.

The Whispered Secrets of Snow

Snowflakes fall like stories spun,
Upon the earth, a quilt begun.
Each secret held in layers deep,
A winter's promise, quiet sleep.

Whispers weave through branches bare,
Tales of seasons, swirling air.
In the hush, a world transformed,
With every flake, new beauty formed.

Curled in corners, shadows creep,
Softly glistening, secrets keep.
Nature pauses, breathes in trust,
In this blanket of crystalline dust.

Listen close, the frost-tinged night,
Bears witness to the purest light.
In every silence, stories flow,
The whispered secrets of the snow.

Glistening Shadows at Dusk

As daylight fades, shadows grow long,
Night drapes the world in velvet song.
Glistening paths where starlight weaves,
In the quiet hum, the heart believes.

The horizon blushes, a fleeting glance,
Where twilight dances, in silvered trance.
Colors deepen, brush strokes bold,
Bringing warmth to the night so cold.

We walk in dreams where echoes soar,
In the fading light, we long for more.
The air is thick with tales untold,
In the night's embrace, we dare be bold.

Each heartbeat pulses, a glowing spark,
Illuminating all that lies in dark.
Glistening shadows whisper and sigh,
At dusk's sweet altar, we learn to fly.

Ethereal Snowfall Stories

Whispers of winter lace the air,
As soft as dreams held in a prayer,
Snowflakes twirl like stories untold,
Each one a treasure, a wonder to behold.

Silent echoes blanket the ground,
In this hush, the world feels unbound,
Every flake has a tale to share,
Of starry nights and frosted air.

Beneath the glow of a silver moon,
Nature's symphony plays a gentle tune,
With each descent, a memory blooms,
In the heart of winter, magic looms.

So let us gather, hearts open wide,
To hear the stories in the snowy tide,
For every flake, a moment divine,
In the dance of snowfall, our souls intertwine.

The Dance of Frosted Breezes

Dancing lightly on a winter's breath,
Frosted breezes whisper of life and death,
They twirl through branches, crisp and bright,
Painting the world in glowing white.

With a soft sigh, they weave through the trees,
Playing hide and seek with the moonlit freeze,
Each gust tells tales of ages past,
Of timeless moments that forever last.

Amidst the chill, there's warmth in the air,
A promise of spring, hidden somewhere,
The dance evolves, a gentle ballet,
Where cold meets warmth in a fleeting sway.

In this frosted waltz, we find our place,
Embracing the beauty, the grace,
For every breeze carries a dream anew,
In the dance of frost, our spirits renew.

Radiance of the Snowbound Wilderness

In the quiet of the snowbound land,
Where whispers dance 'neath frost-kissed trees,
A canvas painted by winter's hand,
Radiates beauty as the spirit frees.

Crystalline glimmers in the pale sunlight,
Each flake a story, each drift a dream,
Nature's soft blanket, serene and bright,
A realm of wonder, a silent gleam.

Birds in the branches sing sweet refrains,
Their melodies carried on crisp, cool air,
While mountains wear their white, frosted chains,

Guardians of secrets in beauty laid bare.

Here in the wild, where the cold winds sigh,
I find my solace, my heart takes flight,
In the radiance where day meets night,
Embraced by nature, my spirit soars high.

Moonlit Secrets of the Frost

When night descends on the frozen glade,
The moon spills silver on shimmering snow,
Secrets of shadows in silence displayed,
Whispers of ancient winds begin to flow.

Beneath the glow of a celestial sphere,
Nature's heart beats in rhythmic grace,
Frosted leaves glisten, and all becomes clear,
As magic dances in each hidden place.

The stars above, like diamonds afloat,
Guide wanderers lost in the tranquil embrace,
Tracing the paths where dreams had once wrote,
In moonlit gardens, they find their space.

Here in the stillness, the world holds its breath,
As every crystal breathes a tale of the past,
In the serenity of life, facing both birth and death,

Moonlit secrets dwell, infinite and vast.

Twilight's Breath of Icy Air

As twilight falls, the world stands still,
A hush blankets the whispering trees,
The icy air, with a hopeful chill,
Invites the heart to hold its ease.

Glimmers of orange in a fading sky,
Paint strokes of beauty on winter's skin,
Where shadows gather and moments lie,
In twilight's breath, new stories begin.

A gentle sigh, as day turns to night,
The first stars awaken in deepening blue,
While frosty fingers weave magic in flight,
Through the landscape kissed by a shimmering
hue.

Lost in the wonder of this fleeting hour,
I breathe in the peace that the dusk doth share,
With every exhale, I feel the flower
Of dreams unfolding in twilight's fair air.

The Hush of Chilling Memories

In the depth of winter, the memories call,
Like echoes trapped in the mirrored sky,
Each chilling breath holds the weight of it all,
As shadows dance and the heart learns to sigh.

Frayed pages turn in the book of the past,
Where laughter lingers in the frosty breeze,
Beneath layers of snow, tender moments cast,
In the hush that follows, the spirit finds peace.

Whispers of friendships that flickered then
glowed,
In the warmth of gatherings lost to the years,
With every flake that gracefully flowed,
Chilling memories unfurl, drawing tears.

Yet from this stillness, I gather my strength,
With love as the light through the depths of
despair,
In the wake of the cold, I will find the length
Of warmth that lives on in the heart's tender care.

Elegy of the Freeze

In the heart of winter's grasp, where shadows
sigh,
A silence deepened, beneath the cerulean sky.
Flakes of white, like whispers, drift softly to
ground,
Each one a memory lost, a moment profound.

Branches ache with weight, in their frozen
embrace,
Time pauses and waits in this shadowed space.
Life stills in the chill, yet the spirit remains,
Echoes of warmth linger, despite winter's chains.

Underneath the blanket, the earth holds its breath,

Crystals weave stories of life and of death.
In the fold of a frost, we are all but a dream,
As the echoes of warmth, like embers, still gleam.

So let us remember this hushed, hollowed night,
For spring will return, bringing colors so bright.
Yet for now, we embrace the soft chill and freeze,

In the elegy whispered among trembling trees.

Ethereal Whisperings of the Cold

The night wraps gently in frost's silver veil,
Echoes of whispers drift soft through the pale.
Breath of the chilly winds weave tales of the
night,
In the shimmering quiet, the world feels so right.

With each breath of cold, secrets float in the air,
Fragrant with longing, of dreams everywhere.
Stars flicker like candles, alight on the deep,
Holding the stories of those lost in sleep.

Through valleys of silence, the echoes conspire,
In the stillness of winter, hearts warm with desire.

As shadows of twilight embrace day's gentle
cease,
The world, wrapped in wonder, finds its serene
peace.

Ethereal whispers, like lace in the sky,
A melody soft, as the moments go by.
In the hush of the cold, where dreams dare to
unfold,
Life's tapestry glimmers, in silver and gold.

The Flickering Breath of Twilight Frost

As twilight cascades its chill over the ground,
The flickering frost brings a delicate sound.
Whispers of evening, soft as a sigh,
Dance on the edges where shadows comply.

Each breath of the frost is a moment, a pause,
The world draped in stillness, as nature
withdraws.
A tapestry woven of white and of blue,
Embracing the dusk with a tender debut.

Stars peek from blankets of deep indigo,
The sighs of the evening, in silence they flow.
With each flicker of breath, night's magic is cast,

Time holds its essence, each heartbeat, a vast.

In the chilling embrace where the twilight holds
sway,
We gather our dreams, bid the day gently sway.
For in the flickering breath of the frost adorned
night,
Lies the beauty of moments, of endings, of light.

Nights Cradled in Crystal Silence

In the cradle of night, where silence takes flight,
Crystal glimmers dance softly, enchanting the
sight.
Wrapped in the darkness, the stars softly glow,
As the world sinks in slumber, the hush gently
flows.

Each heart beat a murmur, a soft, tender call,
In the arms of the night, we are cradled by all.
Frosty tendrils weave stories on windows of
dreams,
In the cold of the night, there's warmth in the
seams.

Underneath a quilt made of whispers and stars,
We find solace together, erasing all scars.
With every soft breath, the silence we weave,
In the crystal-made nights, we learn how to
believe.

So let the world slumber, as silence takes hold,
Each moment wrapped gently in silver and gold.
For in the cradled nights, where the stillness
resides,
We find peace in the softness, where the heart
abides.

Echoes Beneath the Ice

Silent whispers trapped in freezing air,
Echoes wander through the slumbering deep.
Beneath the ice, where shadows softly stare,
Ancient secrets in the coldness keep.

Chasms echo stories long forgot,
Frozen memories in the stillness lie.
Nature's breath, a rhythm, never caught,
The heartbeats of a world that can't say goodbye.

A Dance of Crystal Whispers

In the moonlight's glow, the crystals gleam,
Dancing softly on the winter's breath.
Each flicker a fragment of a frozen dream,
A pirouette of life amid the death.

Branches sway, adorned in glittering lace,
Whispers flutter through the soft, still night.
Nature's orchestra, a delicate embrace,
As silence swells with the beams of light.

Whispering Frost on Bare Branches

Beneath the frosted touch of morning's glow,
Bare branches cradle droplets, pure and bright.
Whispers of winter in the gentle flow,
Each crystal formed beneath the foggy light.

A hush falls heavily across the land,
Nature holds its breath in tranquil grace.
Frosted fingers stretch across the strand,
Whispering secrets in a cold embrace.

The Voice of the Howling Gales

Through the night, the gales begin to wail,
A symphony of shadows, wild and free.
Their haunting echoes tell a somber tale,
An untamed spirit roaming endlessly.

Windswept whispers fill the empty skies,
Each gust a story carried far and wide.
Nature's voice, the truth that never lies,
In the howling gales, the world confides.

Milton Keynes UK
Ingram Content Group UK Ltd.
UKHW022348201024
449848UK00006B/44